Baby Animals

Puppies

ALICE TWINE

PowerKiDS press™

New York

For Gus and Mia Mosle

Published in 2008 by The Rosen Publishing Group, Inc.
29 East 21st Street, New York, NY 10010

First Edition

Editor: Amelie von Zumbusch
Book Design: Julio Gil
Photo Researcher: Nicole Pristash

Photo Credits: Cover, pp. 1, 5, 7, 9, 11, 13, 15, 17, 19, 21, 24 (top left, top right, bottom left, bottom right) Shutterstock.com; p. 23 © www.istockphoto.com/Eileen Hart.

Library of Congress Cataloging-in-Publication Data

Twine, Alice.
  Puppies / Alice Twine. — 1st ed.
      p. cm. — (Baby animals)
  Includes index.
  ISBN 978-1-4042-4143-5 (library binding)
  1. Puppies—Juvenile literature. I. Title.
  SF426.5.T93 2008
  636.7'07—dc22
                                          2007018412

Manufactured in the United States of America.

Contents

Baby dogs are called puppies.

A puppy has four legs, four paws, and a tail. Puppies wag their tail when they are happy.

Some puppies have pointed ears. Other puppies, like this one, have **floppy** ears.

There are many kinds, or breeds, of puppies. This puppy is a **border collie**.

Labradors are one of the best-liked breeds of puppies.

13

Dalmation puppies are born with white fur. After a few weeks, their spots start to form.

Newborn puppies drink their mother's milk. As they grow older, puppies learn to eat out of a bowl.

17

Puppies need lots of sleep.
They sleep between 18 and 20
hours a day.

Puppies love to play. They like to run, jump, and chase things. This puppy is playing with a ball.

Puppies make very good pets. They are friendly and fun to play with. Does anyone you know have a puppy?

Words to Know

border collie

dalmation

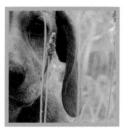
floppy

labrador

Index

Web Sites

Due to the changing nature of Internet links, PowerKids Press has developed an online list of Web sites related to the subject of this book. This site is updated regularly. Please use this link to access the list:
www.powerkidslinks.com/baby/pup/